ISBN 978-0-483-40282-9
PIBN 10093292

THE

TRUE DISCIPLINARIAN

A COURSE OF

PRACTICAL RELIGION

AND

TRAINING FOR THE ETERNAL WORLD,

TOGETHER

WITH THE EXPERIENCE OF THE AUTHOR,
AND REMARKS ON LITURGY.

BY B. M. FRICK, M. D.

No man knoweth the Son, but the Father, neither knoweth
any man the Father save the Son, and he to whomsoever the
Son will reveal him.—MATT. XI. 27.

LANCASTER, PA.:
INQUIRER PRINTING & PUBLISHING CO.
1878.

COPYRIGHTED, 1879,
BY B. M. FRICK, M. D.

INQUIRER P. & P. CO.,
STEREOTYPERS AND PRINTERS,
LANCASTER, PA.

PREFACE.

THE Son of man is come to save that which was lost." Matt. xviii. 11. Therefore the point to arrive at, or the good to be accomplished, to my fellowmen, is their souls' salvation, as the reading of many books is too much labor for the majority of men ; and more so, when we consider the shortness of the memory, and the natural inclination to read about and seek after those things which tend to their external wants. I have therefore tried to explain in a few words (in the way that God hath given me understanding,) the great mysteries of our repentance, conversion and discipline through our life in this world, and our final deliverance from this body, namely, our eternal salvation through Christ Jesus our Lord ;—

leaving altogether out of sight church government, sectarianism, vain disputings, and man's differing in opinions.

THE AUTHOR.

Willow Street, Lancaster Co., Pa.,
Sept. 6th, 1878.

MISCELLANEOUS CONTENTS.

TRUE DISCIPLINARIAN.

PRELIMINARY.

HOW shall a man believe in him whom he doth not know, and how shall a man know, if he is not taught? A certain king asked his counselor, *What is God?* The counselor asked for time till the morrow; on the morrow he appeared and wished three days' more time. "How is this?" saith the King. The answer was, "The more I think about it, the less I know about it." But it is not so with us, unto whom God hath revealed by the Holy Ghost, through Jesus Christ coming into the flesh, and since then unto those who love and serve him by the same spirit;

but the world knoweth him not, because it sees him not.

Acts xvii. 23. "*To the unknown God,* Whom therefore ye ignorantly worship, him declare I unto you"—God that made the world and all things, seeing he is Lord of heaven and earth, and dwelleth not in temples made with hands, as though he needeth any thing, seeing he giveth life and breath and all things, and hath made of one blood all nations of men, for to dwell upon the face of the earth, and has determined the times before appointed and bounds of their habitation, that they should seek the Lord, if haply they might feel after him and find him, though he be not far from every one of us.

Scripture defines God to be a spirit, the Father, Creator and Governor of all things; he is the primary cause, the first cause, the self-existing cause, the only cause, the eternal cause, the great and all-governing cause, of heaven, the earth, the sea, and all that in them is, without beginning and without end, God is a *word* and is *power*.

John i. 1: "In the beginning was the word, and the word was with God, and the word was God ; the same was in the beginning with God. All things were made by him, and without him was not anything made that was made. In him was life ; and the life was the life of man." Isa. xliii. 10-11 : " Believe me, and understand that I am he ; before me there was no God formed, neither shall there be after me. I, even I, am the Lord, and besides me there is no Saviour." No man hath at any time seen God with mortal eyes, save in Jesus Christ when in the flesh ; he hath declared he was the only God ever formed. " He that seeth me, seeth the Father." " I am alpha and omega, the first and the last, the beginning and the end." He did show unto man the almighty *word*, and *power* was in him, by doing the wonderful miracles in the sight of man, declaring unto Jews and Gentiles that the Father was in him, and he in the Father, and that he had power over sin, death and hell, which man hath not, except so far as he has received power from Christ to overcome sin. As many as believed gave he the power to become the children of God.

Now I have tried to explain what is God, and who is God: this then is the first, and the great, and the all-ruling power, and it is good, and there is no evil in it. There is none good but God; he is the great King of kings, and the Lord of lords, and hath all rule and government under him; then if such is the case, there must of necessity be ruling servants under him, to carry out his command and enforce obedience, and punish evil doers.

WHO IS THE DEVIL?

The question is to be answered, There is a secondary power, which had its beginning with *pride* and *ambition*, striving for the supremacy in heaven. Lucifer, an angel of high standing, was the originator of evil; he caused a war among the angels in heaven, and disobedience of the same, but he and his whole host were cast out. He hath become an enemy unto God and all his works; he is now the opposite power; though secondary only, yet hath he a great power, having principalities and rulers under him, (namely, the angels that were cast out with him,) to bring about all manner of evil and destruction upon man, the creature of God, infusing into man to disobey his Creator, causing divisions among themselves, wars and fighting continually. His name is the Evil Spirit, the Devil, Satan, and the Old Serpent, that brought sin, suffering and destruction upon our first parents in the garden of Eden. Let us now consider some of his doings and acts among men. Job i. and ii, we can see the operation of this evil spirit, how he infused or inspired in the minds of the Sabeans to slay Job's servants with the sword, and to take away the oxen and asses as booty, and then caused fire to fall upon the sheep and consume them. Not yet satisfied, he entered into the minds of the Chaldeans, to slay Job's servants with the sword, and carry the camels away; then caused a great storm to rise in the wilderness, and brought it upon the house where Job's sons and daughters were feasting, tore it to pieces and killed them all; and after destroying all that Job had, he was not satisfied, but asked leave to attack his body, and smote him with sore boils, from the crown of his head to the soles of his feet, but his life he had no privilege to touch. (Solomon saith there are two things that never say enough, death and the grave.) Now let us follow him down to Egypt, and see his mighty power exerted over Pharaoh, King of Egypt. As soon as the king acknowledged the supreme power of God and promised to consent to

God's request, he placed his foot upon Satan, and shut off the destroyer, and healed the damage; but so soon as Pharaoh was healed and at ease, the king was inspired by the devil again to act deceitfully, hence another opportunity for destruction was at hand, over the king's affairs; and such were Satan's works carried on through the Ten Plagues of Egypt. Not satisfied with all this, he followed up and destroyed Pharaoh's whole host in the Red Sea. Doth he stop here? No! Follow him on through the whole line of God's people, while traveling in the wilderness. When Moses was withdrawn from the congregation to the top of Mount Sinai, for the purpose of receiving instructions concerning the government of God's people, Satan came in among the people, and infused into their minds to make themselves a golden calf, and fall down before it, and say, "These be the gods that brought us out of the land of Egypt," so as to dishonor God, who was really their deliverer. Here we can plainly see his first sin, *pride* and *ambition*, not willing that God's supremacy should be acknowledged, but acting in opposition all along as time rolled on, causing insurrection, disputing, and disobedience, usurping all power in his might to get the people to do evil, until he had the whole host of God's people destroyed in the wilderness, save two, Caleb and Joshua, being in number over six hundred thousand, beside women and children. Again, when Herod the king was in power, and the King of kings and Saviour of the world was born, he was ready to carry on his fiendish work through Herod, and induced him to slay many innocent children, but failed to accomplish his end. But the greatest work he ever undertook was to tempt Christ—God himself in the flesh—asking him to fall down and worship him. Herein he failed (by his misconception of the work of God to bring about man's salvation.) Satan followed Christ in his opposition until he had accomplished his work (as he thought) by nailing Christ to the cross; but through and by that operation Satan lost all his power over death, and destruction of all those who serve God through Christ. Yes, Satan lost his power over that death of our first parents which he gained through their disobedience to God's command, for "in the day wherein ye eat of it, ye shall surely die." Now we can safely say, there is no more fear of death for all those who walk according to the doctrine of Christ. Since that time we see his work of opposition in the world, in the children of disobedience; how he taketh advantage of every opportunity that can be thought of, to produce havoc and destruction among the children of men, by raising up hurricanes, destructive storms, heavy-rainfalls, hail, thunder and lightning, fire and floods or water, to tear up trees, throw down buildings, and destroy man, beast and vegetation from off the face of the earth ; not satisfied with all this, but infusing into God's people to quarrel and fight and sin.

I have now tried or attempted to explain some of Satan's mighty works, that we may have a little understanding and knowledge of his doings among the children of men; by his fruits ye shall know him.

OUR RESPONSIBILITY.

And now, what shall we do ? Will we sit down in fear, consternation and horror, and behold all this work going on, and allow this secondary power, even Satan, to cause such havoc and destruction in our land and nation, destroying man and beast, women and children, and the souls of men, when the remedy is at hand, yea in our power to prevent, if we but asked the power of him who doth offer it unto us simply by asking him for it ? I say again, what will we do ?—have we no mind, no understanding, no knowledge at all? No? Will we not consider, will we not give a matter of so vast importance any hought at all? Is it possible that man is dead, deaf, dumb, and blind? can he not be aroused from this great carelessness? can he not be brought to halt and think again? Is it possible? is it possible? But every one goeth after his own business, the farmer to his farm, the carpenter to the house he is building, the blacksmith to fire and anvil, the laborer to his labor, the merchant to his merchandise, the professional man to his office; rulers and governors sit in their chairs considering the responsibilities pertaining to their offices;—all considering how they may live so as to gather money and riches, and yet appear before man honorable and of high standing, forgetting God as the last thing to be noticed; and when Satan bringeth forth his mighty destructions and devastation by raising up black clouds, flashing of fire, heavy peals of thunder and mighty storms, black-

2

ness and darkness come rolling on unexpectedly; then, and only then, will men rise up from off their seats and occupations, wherein they were so busily engaged, with fear and trembling facing the horrible destruction coming upon them, their bodies cast down in death, for to appear before whom they shall give an account of their doings and of their discipline and training for the eternal world, in this their time allotted unto them, for the glorification of their Creator and the Preserver of all things. But now no thought has been taken about God and eternal things, hence they are not prepared for the work now before them. What shall we say? Had no time? Did not know what God required? Did you not see it with your eyes, hear it with your ears, and understand it with your heart, what God required of you? Is it possible that this is a true picture for God and man to behold? No wonder did David say, "Oh! that mine eyes were fountains of water, and my cheeks were valleys, that I might weep, that the tears might flow down my cheeks like rivers of water.'' Now if this is the true state and condition of God, man, and Satan, why and wherefore is it so? We say, these things must needs be so; if there is to be a governor or ruler, there must needs be a commandment, or we would be all alike; and if command is given by a supreme ruler unto his subjects, there must be a penalty attached to prevent the violation of the same; then must there be of necessity one to carry out or inflict the punishment attached. If this were not the case, man would have no will of his own; he would be no free agent. We read that even the angels in heaven are not slaves bound unto God, but have the power of volition, to obey or not to obey; and man is placed on equality with angels in this respect. Yet say you, man has fallen from his original state: so have the angels. Lucifer, a great

prince in heaven, with one-third part of the
angels at that time, have fallen, and we read
they are bound in eternal chains of darkness,
unto the day of final settlement of all things,
when they shall receive their reward with
those men who embrace not the opportunity
to be saved in the time given unto them;
but those fallen angels are not on salvable
ground, like man is, for whom provision was
made.   Now, we say man is more highly favored with God than even the angels are in
this respect, because he answered a two-fold
purpose for God's work.   Man is of great
service to God in this world.   What would
this world be if there was no man in it?
Consider how it would appear.   To what
purpose would the earth be? what pleasure
would there be to its Creator, with all the
glories and powers in it, if there was no man
upon the face of it, just as he is made, with
hands to labor, feet to walk, eyes to see,
ears to hear, and a mind to understand—yea,

a great mind, to consider all things that are
and all that therein is? And on the other
necessary to be done in this glorious earth
hand man hath an eternal spirit, to glorify
God in the eternal world to come, after this
earthly work is ended.

REDEMPTION.

Who has ever made anything to his own
pleasure and satisfaction, that does not love
it, would not remedy its defects, and set it
aright, for his own satisfaction and pleasure?
So God hath created man in his own image
and likeness, with the power of volition to
will for himself, that he should be no slave or
servant, but a son, who should be co-equal
with himself in the great business and enjoyment throughout the eternal world. Now
if we could but understand the near kin and
relationship we hold toward God, and the
love he bears toward us as his creatures by
this sacred tie; we are bone of his bone and
flesh of his flesh, which he hath proved unto

us by coming into the flesh and doing for us that which we were not able to do in the state and condition we had placed ourselves, because we did give way and sinned against his command, and fell under the power of Satan (by our own actions), who held us in captivity and bondage, until he came himself into the flesh, and fulfilled that law which his justice would not otherwise but demand. To keep his original justice, and abide in the truth, he therefore came down in his mighty power, fulfilled that law to the letter without sin, and then died the death in our stead, namely the death of a sinner; for he called out " My God, my God, why hast thou forsaken me?" So he paid our penalty, that divine justice may abide and he can have mercy upon us, namely the forgiveness of our sin. Justice and truth is not injured if we claim him for our righteousness.

It matters not how merciful and unwilling to mete out a punishment; when there is a decree that altereth not, or that cannot be broken without the loss of his own steadfastness and of justice and truth, it must be positively enforced, however unwilling. For example, there was a certain king who passed a decree, that for a certain offence the ofender's eyes were to be put out; and the one that committed the offence, was the king's own son. What was to be done? The king had to make a sacrifice, or fall from his own steadfastness, and become a trifler. He therefore proposed that one of his eyes should be put out and one of his son's, so that he might show his subjects the unalterableness of the king's law and command. Again, how was it with Darius, the king in Daniel's time? If there could have been a remedy found to rescue Daniel, it would have been surely done; for the king worked hard until the going down of the sun—yes, all day—to find out how he might rescue Daniel from being cast into the lions' den. There is no doubt the king shed many tears; but there was no help, the decree altered not.

In such a condition and position man placed God by his own action. What is to be done? It matters not how unwilling God is in Christ Jesus; he cannot save man in any other way than that which is laid down. He calleth upon all men everywhere, saying, " Turn ye, oh! why will you die." It is not His will that any should perish, but that all should consent, and escape the punishment which might follow. Thus, we say, it is such a decree that altereth not. God saith himself, what more can I do, that I have not done?—having himself suffered our penalty upon the cross—and calleth us to render up our will and come and be saved, the only way in which he can save us.

John i. 29 to 35: " The next day John seeth Jesus coming unto him, and saith, Behold the Lamb of God which taketh away the sin of the world; this is he of whom I said,

after me cometh a Man which is preferred before me ; for he was before me.   And I knew
him not, but that he should be made manifest to Israel, therefore am I come baptizing
with water.   And John bare record, saying,
I saw the Spirit descending for heaven like a
dove, and it abode upon him.   And I knew
him not; but he that sent me to baptize with
water, the same said unto me, Upon whom
thou shalt see the Spirit descending and
remaining on him, the same is he which
baptizeth with the Holy Ghost.   And I saw,
and bare record that this is the Son of God.''

Again, Luke iv. 16 to 18: '' And he came
to Nazareth, where he had been brought up ;
and, as his custom was, he went into the syn-
agogue on the Sabbath day, and stood up for
to read.   And there was delivered unto him
the Book of the Prophet Esaias.   And when
he had opened the Book, he found the place
where it was written, The spirit of the Lord
is upon me, because he hath anointed me to

preach the gospel to the poor; he hath sent me to heal the broken-hearted, to preach deliverance to the captives, and recovering of sight to the blind, to set at liberty them that are bruised."

Mark i. 15: "And saying, The time is fulfilled, and the kingdom of God is at hand; repent ye, and believe the gospel."

Matt. iv. 17: "From that time Jesus began to preach, and to say, Repent, for the kingdom of heaven is at hand."

Acts xvii. 29 to 31: "For as much then as we are the offspring of God, we ought not to think that the God-head is like unto gold, or silver, or stone, graven by art and man's device. And the times of this ignorance God winked at; but now commandeth he all men everywhere to repent; because he hath appointed a day, in the which he will judge the world in righteousness by that man whom he hath ordained; wherein he hath given assurance unto all men, in that he hath raised him from the dead."

In concluding the preliminary part, we we must say all is right, and just, and good, and necessary so to be. God alone is wise, and He alone hath understanding of His great and mighty works. We must say, God is in his proper place, angels are in their proper place, man is in his proper place, Christ is in his proper place, Satan is in his proper place, and the salvation of man through Christ is in its proper place. If we consider all the circumstances, we must say yea and amen ; so it was from the beginning, so be it in the end ; and this alone grieves me, that I have so sinned against the Lord my God.

REPENTANCE.

REPENTANCE implies that a certain measure of divine wisdom is communicated to the sinner, and he thereby becomes wise unto salvation; it means sorrow for sins which are past, a remembrance or after-thought of a misspent life, producing an uneasiness of the mind, upon a consideration of what is done. There is still remaining in the human mind a part of God's light of original righteousness; man hath died the death of the power to do that which is right, yet there is a spark of light left remaining, so that man knoweth when he doeth wrong; and this proves itself to be a fact, for the child one or more years old knoweth when it does wrong before father or mother tell him of it; experience teaches this, and Satan said, You shall not surely die, but shall be wise as gods, knowing

good from evil. The Saviour, speaking of
man's final apostasy, says, And if that light
that in thee be darkness, how great will that
darkness be! Thus we travel on with this
knowledge in us, until a special effort is
made by the Spirit of God, the Holy
Ghost, so that we are compelled to hear
his voice, riveting mighty convictions on us
of our sins; so much so that there is no rest
in us, neither by day nor by night, on account
of our sins; but we are not willing to surren-
der, and wish to get rid of this trouble, not
by repentance, but by seeking worldly jollity,
often the wine-cup, and such company as is
not under such influence, to work this trouble
off. Oh; what obstinacy is in man! But the
voice of God is, when you hear his voice harden not your heart. Such, then, is a special
call to repentance; and if you harden your
heart, and fight against the Spirit of God,
you may never have another chance to repent; because man cannot repent when he

pleases, but when God gives him the power to repent only; for he saith, "How long, ye simple ones, will you love simplicity, ye scorners delight in your scornings, and fools hate knowledge? Turn ye at my reproof. Behold, I will pour out my spirit upon you, and will make known my words unto you, now, because I have called and you refused, I have stretched out my hand and you did not regard, and took none of mine reproof, and set at naught my counsel, I also will laugh at your calamity, and will mock when your fear cometh." As far as my experience goes, man, or some men, will have three or four special calls to repentance during their lifetime; therefore greatly fear lest God's spirit will take its flight, and then there will be no more saving repentance left for thee. How many have gone distracted, and committed suicide, to get out of trouble!

But there are various kinds of repentance mentioned in Scripture, and we can see the fruits of it. We read of the beast in the Revelation that had a deadly wound and was made whole, and all that were not of God worshiped the beast; and of that great city that became a cage for every foul beast and unclean bird. First, natural repentance, or that which is merely from a natural conscience. Second, a national repentance, such as the Jews in Babylon were called up to, to which temporal blessings were promised; Ezekiel—"Therefore I will judge you, O house of Israel, every one according to his way, saith the Lord. Repent and turn yourselves from all your transgression whereby you have transgressed, and make a new heart, and a new spirit; for why will you die, O house of Israel? for I have no pleasure of him that dieth, saith the Lord God; wherefore turn yourselves and live." Third, an external repentance, or outward humiliation for sin, as in the case of Ahab; he went into his house and laid on his bed, turned his face to

the wall and would not eat bread, because
he could not have things as he desired.
Fourth, a hypocritical repentance, as repre-
sented in Ephraim—"Though I have bound
and strengthened their arms, yet they
imagine mischief against me. They return,
but not unto the most high; they are like a
deceitful bow. Their princes shall fall by
the sword, for the rage of their tongue; this
shall be their derision in the land of Egypt.
Fifth, a legal repentance, which is a main
work of the law, and the effects of conviction
of sin by it, which in time will wear off and
come to nothing. Sixth, an evangelical repentance, which consists in conviction of sin,
confession of it, hatred to it, and renuncia-
tion of it. A legal repentance and an evangelical can be distinguished thus : First, a
legal repentance is from a sense of danger
and a fear of wrath; an evangelical is a true
mourning for sin, and an earnest desire to be
delivered from sin. Second, a legal repent-

ance flows from the fear of punishment threatened, and in unbelief; an evangelical is always the fruit and consequence of a saving faith. Third, a legal repentance flows from aversion, hatred or dislike to God and his holy law; but an evangelical from love to both. Fourth, a legal repentance flows from discouragement and despondency; but an evangelical from an encouraging hope. Fifth, a legal repentance is temporary; but an evangelical is a daily exercise of the true Christian. Sixth, a legal repentance doth at most produce a partial external reformation; but an evangelical is a total change of our heart and life. The author of repentance is God, the subject the sinner. None but those who have sinned can repent. Though many have, no doubt, repeatedly felt smart pain in their conscience, and endeavored to quiet it with a few such aspirations as these—Lord have mercy upon me; Lord forgive me, and lay not this sin to my charge, for Christ's sake;

—and thus of the work of repentance they know little; they have not suffered the pangs of conscience to form themselves into true repentance; a deep conviction of their lost and ruined state both by nature and practice of sin, and contrition for sin, have only had a superficial influence upon their hearts; their repentance is not a deep, radical work; they have not suffered themselves to be led into the various chambers of the house of imagery, to detect the hidden abominations everywhere set up, against the honor of God and the safety of their souls; when they have felt a little smarting from a wound of sin, they have it slightly healed, and their repentance is that from which they may repent; it was partial and inefficient, and its end proves it; they walk straight before man and greatly fear man, but do not consider God, who considereth the desires and intents of the heart, the inward man; they have not, through the excess of sorrow for sin, fled to lay hold upon

the hope that is set before them, and refused
to be comforted until they felt that word pow-
erfully spoken into their hearts, "Son or
daughter, be of good cheer, thy sins are forgiven thee." No man should consider his
repentance as having answered a saving end
to his soul, till he feels that God, for Christ's
sake, hath forgiven his sins, and the spirit of
God testifies to his spirit that he is accepted,
and a child of God. How few generally
confess their own sin! They see not their
guilt; they are continually making excuses
for their crimes—the strength and sub-
tility of the tempter, the natural weakness of
their minds, the unfavorable circumstances in
which they are placed, etc., etc., are all
pleaded as excuses for their sins, and possi-
bility of repentance is shut out or prevented;
for until a man take his sin to himself, until
he acknowledge that he alone is guilty, he
cannot be humbled, and consequently cannot
be saved. Reader, until thou own thyself and

thyself only, and feel that thou alone, art re-
sponsible for all thy iniquities, there is no
hope for thy salvation. Reader, learn that
true repentance is work, and not the work of
an hour; it is not passing regret, but a deep
and alarming conviction that thou art a
fallen spirit, hast broken God's law, art under
the curse and in danger of hell fire. He
who seeth his inward parts in God's light, or
as God seeth him, need not transgress and
sin any more to produce penitence and contrition for sin, for he feels too much already to
give his will to sin more. As the apostle saith,
we are not under the law, and if sin abound
grace doth still more abound, therefore we
may sin that grace may abound; but the
answer is, How shall we sin who are dead
unto sin ?—and this is the death that a man
dies when he steps out of sin into the grace of
Jesus Christ. This is true evangelical repentance. He that sinneth is of the devil, James
saith.

I will give you my own experience of repentance. When I was quite young, I was conscious that God was not pleased with me on account of my sins; and when I was seven years old I went to school, the first session of which, three months in a year, called a quarter, I took up the German and learned to read well; and then took up the English and learned to read. The first quarter the Bible and Testament were our high school books. (There were no Sunday-schools in those days, at least not away from the city; in fact, we knew nothing about Sabbath-schools in 1825. My parents were members of the Mennonite persuasion.) In this way I became acquainted with the Scriptures. So I lived until I was about sixteen, still conscious that if I were to die my soul would be eternally lost, and consequently greatly fearing death; and when I was about sixteen I had a powerful call to repentance, through the spirit of God. I prayed much, wept much, and read much in the Testament, and was much cast down on account of my lost state and condition through sin ; went to Church, heard preaching with great desire and eagerness. Now there was a woods or grove not far from the house where I lived, in which there was a knob of hill or peak ; thither I frequently resorted after night, so that no one would see me. I prayed and wept much and often, for pardon and forgiveness of my sins ; but all this was a great secret ; I did not wish that any person should know anything about my trouble. Then, after harvest some time, I concluded that I would go up into the mountains, because I had read that Christ often went up into the mountains to pray, and there I thought I could fast and pray without any person to disturb me ; so I started in the evening when it was already dark. I let no one know anything about my going away—I traveled through the fields and along the highway; on reaching the hill country I selected a high peak, there being no public road near; but I could see far over the country—see the people at work in their fields at a great distance. There I commenced reading, praying and weeping alternately (with quite a satisfaction—there being no one to disturb me), which I could do without any effort on my part, for my sorrows were great on account of my sins; and thus I read, wept and prayed, fasting day and night; sometimes I would fall asleep, being worried out, then when awake go to work again, for three nights and days. After three days and nights were thus spent in weeping, praying, reading and fasting, I felt easier on account of my sins; but now, to live right was the next. I was very weak, and felt if I wanted to live I must get something to eat and drink; so I concluded that I would go to a certain bishop whom I had known for some time, and abide with him for some time to learn to live so as to sin no more,

for sin I dreaded greatly. So I left the peak
with my book under my arm, and the first
house I came to I asked for a piece of dry
bread, which I received thankfully. I went
to the pump, ate and drank; now I was ready
for the journey, some fifteen miles. I reached
the Bishop's house, inquired for work, which
was granted. He did not know me, and took
very little notice of me, and the first day I
lost confidence in him on account of a small
act. We were hauling out manure, and we
had it cut down as we loaded it; one of the
cows climbed up where we had it cut straight,
and he expressed such anger, and ran the an-
imal down so furiously, that I could see that
he was a servant of sin, and good could not
be learned from him. After three days I
concluded that he had no power to overcome
evil, and I asked my leave, which was
granted; then I went to the place where I had
left when I went into the mountains; the
man asked me no questions that I remember

of my whereabouts; I told him that I would work on as I did before. All was right as far as I could learn, so I worked, attended the church, and lived really a holy life.

That fall there was a campmeeting near by, which I attended every night and over Sunday; there was the first time that I ever saw the full effects of baptism of fire and the Holy Ghost. I watched very closely, but could not understand anything about it; while others worked, I did not know what to think; but mock I would not, for I feared God. Soon after I changed my place and went into another neighborhood and among ungodly people, who would laugh at my solemn ways and serious living, and did gradually draw me into worldly enjoyments and away from God. All this time I did not confess Christ before man, and had my religion to myself; therefore Christ would not support me; he demands a confession before man. Now my lot fell into another neigh-

borhood among a better people; then I was
called again from within and without, and
becoming acquainted with the church people,
I undertook to confess Christ openly; then
I was baptized and taken into church fellowship. I then traveled with the young, till
I made acquaintance with the one who afterward became my partner in life; she now became a member of the same persuasion
in which her parents and mine held their
church membership, and we did not very long
live as Christians ought to live, and were
thus partakers at the Lord's table, until I was
so sorely condemned that I could no longer
remain in church fellowship, lest I should
eat and drink damnation to my soul by eating and drinking unworthily, not discerning
the Lord's body that it is holy, and none but
the holy dare touch it. Expose my partner
I would not, so I went out into worldly enjoyments to kill sorrow, as is usually the way
with most men; and when I was admonished

I demanded my withdrawal from church fellowship, stating that I was unworthy, and it
was granted. Now was I loose from the
church, and soon loose from God. I now fell
into more gross and worse sins than I ever was
guilty of before, and thus lived quite in loose-
ness and wantonness, and fell into damnable
sins, and lived therein for a long time. I
was as it were blind, having eyes and seeing
not, ears and hearing not, and a mind and
considering not, and the business I was in
was very favorable to such a life.

Now under all this dreadful life God did
not wish to let me be lost, and he did once
more give me a chance to repent; so I was
brought once more to feel my lost state and
condition, and with a view to reformation I
joined the secret orders, which made me
think still more seriously about my latter end,
through that which I was taught and promised in the various ceremonies; God still
pressing more closely upon me the necessity

of my repentance and change of my life. As
I was a great lover of music, I happened to
come where a religious revival was going on,
and I became interested in their singing the
songs of Zion, and of God, and of praise,
and of the acknowledgment of God in
Christ Jesus. I became so much attached to
these that I had much pleasure. but without
really considering what I was singing. I
heard their mighty and earnest prayers to
God to draw sinners to repentance and save
their souls through Christ. I all at once, as
it were, became very sick about my sins, so
that I began to pray in secret again and found
some relief, and formed a hope and anchor
to trust in God. But it was not long until
one day I was in the city of Lancaster,
when a heavy gust came up ; the lightning
flashed vividly, with heavy peals of thunder
following, shaking everything around us. I
and two acquaintances were in their store.
Such lightning, heavy thunder and rain, I had

not seen for many days before, if ever; and as the vivid flashes went through the room, as it were, one of them turned pale and trembled at the awful sight. I, as it were, scorned, and thought, how hard is it to have no hope in God; but I was soon brought to feel that I also was but a sinner, and ready for God's wrath to destroy me. I was consciously reminded when I got home after the shower; the lightning had struck my barn, and killed a valuable horse; shattered the building in a fearful manner, but did not burn it; stunned my wife and the children in her lap severely. Then all my sins returned on me, more than ever; I was made conscious that the wrath of God was over me, and if I did not return he would cut me down and give my portion, which I had long ago justly deserved, even eternal punishment; so I was brought plainly to see that God was just and right to give me my reward, but was still waiting for my return, that I might escape the awful punishment. In considering his long-suffering and my dreadful sins, I was made very sick, and brought to love God for the great mercy that still spared my unworthy life; so I attended the revival meetings very regularly, helped them sing those songs; but I was stopped, seeing it was not true what I was singing. Now I got into great trouble. I could not get rest neither day or night, on account of my great and mighty sins, which now I viewed as being above all measure. I was made conscious if I would not come out openly and with full purpose of heart, he would certainly cut me down. Now the world appeared in mourning; the sun did no more shine in brilliancy; the green vegetation appeared to have lost its color; trees, man and beast appeared to look cast down and sorrowful; I could not eat, sleep, or find rest anywhere; so I was living for a time, not fit to attend to business, wept much, prayed much, but all in secret; Satan would still say, Only let no man know it. Yes, this was worse than death to suffer; then I could say with David, "I am poor and needy, my heart is wounded within me, I am gone like a shadow when it declineth, I am tossed up and down as the locust, my knees are weak through fasting, and my flesh faileth fatness; the sorrows of death compassed me, and the pains of hell got hold of me; I found trouble and sorrow. O Lord, I beseech thee, deliver my soul."

Willing to do anything to get out of this dreadful trouble, I made up my mind to go out to the mourners' bench, as it was called, and seek relief; but the men carrying on the meeting did not know anything about my feelings, at least they never said anything to me about seeking religion. Thus, with the load of condemnation, I attended the meeting every night, saying to myself, Now I will go out and confess my sins unto the Lord. Then the devil would say, Not to-night; wait a little, at least till to-morrow night; it is nearly over now. So I continued in this awful condition for several days and nights, when I would say to myself, O, fool that I was, why did I not jump up and go out when I had the chance ; so I was almost worried to death, through days and nights, between the chances to get out publicly, which seemed to be the only remedy left for me ; for where I would not go, there seemed to be the only place for me to go for relief. I formerly despised such a way as that, but now I found there was no remedy, but go there I must. All this time I was secretly praying, weeping, and mourning to be delivered from this death ; so one night, Satan said, "wait a while," until he had almost cheated me out of the evening again, when I, as it were, gathered all the power within me, jumped up and went out, kneeled down at the bench with all this mighty load of sin upon me, prayed and wept the remaining part of the evening. After the evening's exercises were over, I was told to keep praying earnestly to God to pardon my transgression and forgive my sins for Christ's sake; on the second night I had no difficulty to go out; as soon as the exercise was begun and an invitation given, I went out without any trouble about waiting a little. Now on the second night, while I was praying, weeping and mourning to be delivered from this dreadful lost state and condition, the heaven above me, as it were, became lighted up, and I began to feel easy and good; I could thank and praise God for removing this horrible feeling from me. Then I began to consider, if I now go out among my former companions and they lead me into sin again, what would become of me then; and while I was thinking about this matter (still kneeling at the bench), the whole trouble and sorrow and burden came back in full power; so I fell to praying, weeping and mourning again, until the close of the evening's exercise, feeling no better than I did in the beginning of the evening. Then one of the brethren came to me, and asked how I felt now; I answered, "Not well." "You had been free to-night one time, for I saw it in your countenance." My reply was, "Yes; but while I was thinking about the future life all left me again— about the danger of falling into sin again." "Why," saith he, "you must trust in the Lord; he can keep you, you cannot keep yourself;" which truth I had experienced on former occasions. So he said, "Pray on and labor, and if God gives you clear again, rise up and thank and praise him and cast your care upon him, for he cares for you." Then I went home, lamented, prayed and labored with God on account of my sins, until the third night. I went out to the bench again, prayed, wept, asked God to remove this burden from me for Christ's sake; and when near the close of the evening's exercise, all at

once God took away the black clouds over-
hanging me, and set me free, and showed me
the brightness and glory. All my burden and
sorrow was removed; I felt happy and good.
Now there was no more condemnation resting upon me, so I got up, and thanked and
praised God for my deliverance. Now I
could sing in the spirit and with the understanding also; now it was true that which I
sung; I could sing now, I love Jesus and he
loves me; he was now *my* Jesus, because he
died for me, died that I might live. Now
heaven appeared a new heaven, the earth a
new earth, and God in Christ Jesus pleasant
for me to behold. There was no more condemnation, no dread and fear of the wrath
of God; all had passed away, life was sweet
unto me; the grass, the trees, appeared once
more in their living green; the sun returned
in its full splendor and glory; men, women
and children appeared to be happy. I
thought even the cattle, fowls and birds in

the air appeared to rejoice; labor went easy; when I went out at night and beheld the starry heaven, its great ruler appeared to smile. The Saviour saith, the angels rejoice over one sinner that repents. I felt light like a feather; would not stumble at anything in the dark, because all was life and joy and peace; I was strong. Glory to God in the highest when I think of that time, that happy day when Jesus washed my sins away. I was divorced from the world, and married to God through Christ. Well may the poet say :

> "O, how happy are they,
>   Who their Saviour obey,
>   And have laid up their treasures **above**;
>   Tongue cannot express
>   The sweet comfort and peace,
>   Of a soul in its earliest love.
>   Say, will you to Mount Zion go?
>   Say, will you have this Christ or no?"

As a first and natural aim, all men do seek

after happiness and enjoyment in this life; but take it for granted that there is no real happiness and enjoyment found in this world outside of the religion of Jesus Christ. There is still and again a continued emptiness or void in the mind and soul, of man, that cannot be supplied without repentance and faith in the Lord Jesus Christ. Faith cometh by hearing. Reader, now may God bless you to find that which you labor so much to find, namely, enjoyment and happiness in this life; but take it for granted that you cannot find it, unless you learn to know the only true and living God, and Jesus Christ whom he has sent to save the poor and fallen creature, man. This is eternal life, to know thee, the only true and living God. God saith unto you, Come and try me, and see if I will not open the windows of heaven and pour out such a blessing that there will not be room to contain it.

Now, before closing this part of our little

work, let me caution you, sinners and inexperienced professors of religion, if any such read this, that you do not mock or speak against these things, because you cannot understand them ; but fear God, in whose hand and power your life and soul is: for when I thought I did know some things, I could not understand when I saw with mine own eyes the baptism of fire and the Holy Ghost. As a matter of course, I saw the effects only. I did know a certain preacher who saw these effects often, of the outpouring of God's Spirit and that on many, and expressed himself in these words, "We know that this is not the Spirit of God." Whose spirit then could it have been ? We know that they accused Christ of having a devil, and casting out the evil spirits through Beelzebub, the prince of devils ; you may read what follows. I told him I would not for all the world say that, and he should never say it again; and I suppose he never did, for he was shortly afterward struck down and died. God did silence his tongue for ever in this world. Now that every one must be exercised in their repentance as I was in all things, let no one think, because experience teaches differently ; but this must be true, that no one can be found that was not lost, and no one can repent that is not a sinner. Christ did not come to call the righteous, but sinners to repentance. To save that which was lost, such was his mission, such is his purpose now, and such will it be till the end of time ; and a man's repentance is not finished until he finds his peace with God ; if he falls into sin he must repent again, if God gives him the power to do it. And God had mercy upon me, for I had not received the Holy Ghost; only since my last repentance, I was repeatedly baptized with it. God the Father is the power, Jesus Christ is the intercessor, and the Holy Ghost is the messenger that conveys and reveals what hath been accomplished in the courts of heaven to the penitent. Christ's own words are : " Ye must be born again ;" " Except a man is born again he cannot see the kingdom of heaven," or of God ; and again, "Except a man is born of water and the spirit, he cannot *enter into* the kingdom of God." *Forget it not, forget it not.*

PART SECOND.

DISCIPLINE AND TRAINING FOR THE ETERNAL WORLD.

NOW we are justified, now we are converted, now we are regenerated and sanctified in our minds, we are born again through the power of the spirit of God; now we know that we have passed from death unto life, because we love the brethren (that is, the people of God); for he that is begotten loveth them that are begotten, for we are divorced from the world and are espoused unto Jesus Christ, for through him have we found our peace with God. Now all is love, all is joy, peace and happiness. We think we can never displease God and Christ any more for ever. Thus we travel on for sometime, without carefulness, because God is all

and in all.   We take no scrip, no purse, no
shoes, neither sword with us, nor is anything
wanting; for God is with us, and we do as
occasion serves us.   We cannot mourn, because the Bridegroom is with us.   We are
like unto a new-married pair according to the
flesh; they travel on in joy, in peace and happiness, having no knowledge at all of the difficulties, conflicts, trials, sorrows and sufferings, and the various disappointments that
they will meet through after life.   Again,
we are as an infant, that hath every thing
done by its parents that is required, and is
held safely in its mother's lap, knowing no
wants, but all is peace and joy.   But now
cometh the washing of regeneration by and
through the word of God; and this is a great
work, to put off the old man, who is defiled
through lust and ignorance, and to put on
the new man, who is formed after the image
of God, in righteousness and true holiness.
Jesus said, "When I sent you out, ye wanted

nothing; but now, he that hath a purse let him take it, and likewise his scrip; and he that hath no sword, let him sell his garment and buy one. God in early days spoke through the prophet about this work, Proclaim ye among the Gentiles, prepare war, wake up the mighty men, let all the men of war draw near, beat your plough-shares into swords, and your pruning-hooks into spears; let the weak say, I am strong" (to fight the battle of the Lord). Jesus saith, " Ye which have followed me in the regeneration, when the Son of Man shall sit on the throne of his glory, ye also shall sit upon twelve thrones, judging the twelves tribes of Israel."

Now, if we review man naturally, we find he was born a child, and grows up to boyhood, then to a young man, and some to old fathers and mothers. We ask not of a child that which belongs to boyhood, neither of a boy that which belongs to a man, nor of young men that which belongs to old fathers and mothers; for their various capacities or abilities have not come to maturity; they will be accomplished and taught during the number of their years. So likewise is man exercised by divine grace; hence cometh the doctrine of concision; of such it is said we should beware. Finally, my brethren, rejoice in the Lord; to write the same thing indeed is not grievous, but to you it is safe; beware of dogs, beware of evil workers, beware of the concision. Now, who are dogs but those who bark at every person and everything but their own?—and this is the nature of dogs, one barking will set all the dogs barking in a neighborhood. Who are the evil workers, but those who select passages of Scripture, to carry out their vain minds, and cause divisions and disputings with vain babblings, and neglect the more important work, to have their peace with God through Christ, and walk with him in fear and humility? Who are of the concision, but such as are mentioned in holy writ?—they said, get thee away, I am holy and thou art a sinner; I am right, but thou art in error. God by the prophet saith, such are as smoke to the eyes and brimstone to the nostrils; mark all things that are written for the man of God, and do that which is in thy power to do with thy might; but if thou do these things to be saved they will not save thee, and if thou do them not thou wilt not be saved. Thou art inexcusable, O man, whosoever thou art that judgest another, for in that thou judgest another thou condemnest thyself; or despisest thou the long suffering of God, not knowing that the goodness of God leadeth thee to repentance? And if thou art no vain person nor open sinner, know this, that thou hast no righteousness of thine own to save thee, for if thou hast any righteousness it is of the Lord; thou didst receive it, namely, the power of the Lord to overcome sin. Be thankful therefore, and be not high minded.

· Love is stronger than death. This **was** frequently exhibited by the first Christians, and many escaped further discipline and training, by being cut off and received into glory in their first love. What workings, what sufferings, what sorrows, what conflicts and prayers to God, had the Apostle Paul with his children, until Christ was formed in them, as he called it ! No wonder he spoke of the sin that so easily beset us, which would say, Let them alone ; they are attached to their idols ; why should I labor any longer? I am the Lord's, — forgetting that we too are saved by Jesus Christ only, and if so be that we have received a goodly portion of grace, it is to benefit others and not ourselves only. O, that God would give us wisdom and an understanding heart ; yea, I say, who can see the great and mysterious works of God?— tongue cannot express that which we do know, and we see that we know nothing at all yet of what we ought to know.

My son, if thou come to serve the Lord, prepare thy soul for temptation, set thy heart aright, and constantly endure, and make not haste in the time of trouble. Cleave to the Lord, and depart not from his precepts, that thou mayest be increased at the latter end. Whatever is brought upon thee, take it cheerfully, and be patient. When thou art changed to a low estate—for gold is tried in the fire, and acceptable men in the furnace of adversity—believe in him, and he will help thee; order thy way aright and trust in him; ye that fear the Lord, wait for his mercy; go not aside, lest ye fall; believe in him, and your reward shall not fail. He that feareth the Lord will honor his father, and do service to his parents as to his masters. Again, honor thy father and mother, both in word and in deed; for the blessing of the father establishes the houses of the children, but the curse of the mother rooteth out foundations. For death and bloodshed,

strife and sword, calamities, famine, tribula-
tion and the scourge, are created for the dis-
obedient and wicked, and for their sakes the
flood came. Fire and water, thunder and
lightning, storm and hail and wild beasts,
shall destroy the wicked, but it shall not
come near the righteous; therefore fear to be
wicked.

Now unto those who are of the household
of faith, and in the religion of Jesus Christ,
I would say with the apostle, I would that
you knew what great conflict I have for you
(although you have not seen my face according to the flesh, and probably never will),
that God will have mercy upon you, to keep
your minds through Christ unto full salvation, so that we may not measure ourselves
by ourselves, neither by other brothers and
sisters, nor in any church, but walk honor-
ably and uprightly before God in Christ Jesus,
in whom are hid all the treasures of wisdom
and knowledge; and glory in the Lord, to

seek to do that which is well pleasing in his
sight; for indeed the spirit is willing, but the
flesh is weak; but God hath promised to be
mighty in the weak; and now, if we have
risen with Christ, we seek those things which
are above, where Christ sitteth at the right
hand of God. We set our affections on
things above, and not on things on the earth,
tor we are dead, and our life is hid with
Christ in God. When he who is our life
shall appear, then shall we also appear with
him in glory. Then let us mortify our members which are upon the earth, from fornica-
tion, uncleanness, inordinate affections, evil
lusts, and covetousness which is idolatry, for
which thing's sake the wrath of God cometh
on the children of disobedience; in the
which we walked also at one time, when we
lived in them. But now let us put off all
these, anger, wrath, malice, blasphemy, filthy
communication out of our mouth; lie not one
to another, lest our peace be marred, seeing

we have put off the old man with his deeds,
and have put on the new man, which is renewed in knowledge after him that created
him, where there is neither Greek nor Jew,
circumcision nor uncircumcision, Barbarian,
Scythian, bond or free, but Christ is all and
in all.   Put on therefore, as the elect of God,
holy and beloved, bowels of mercy, kindness,
humbleness of mind, meekness, forbearing
one another, and forgiving one another; if
any have a quarrel against any, even as
Christ forgave us, so let us forgive one
another; and above all these things put on
charity, which is the bond of perfectness,
and let the peace of God rule in our hearts,
to the which we are called into one body
(indeed invisible to the sight of man, but vis-
ible in the sight of God, and to prove this we
need only to refer to Elias the prophet, who
had knowledge far above us, yet he could not
see God's elect people); and be ye thankful.
Let the word of Christ dwell in us richly in

all wisdom, teaching and admonishing one another in psalms and hymns, and spiritual songs, singing with grace in our hearts to the Lord; and whatsoever we do, in word or deed, we do all in the name of the Lord Jesus, giving thanks to God and the father by him. Wives, submit yourselves unto your own husbands, as it is fit in the Lord; husbands, love your wives, and be not bitter against them; children, obey your parents in all things, for this is well pleasing unto the Lord; fathers, provoke not your children to anger, lest they should be discouraged; servants, obey in all things your masters according to the flesh, not with eye-service as men pleasers, but with singleness of heart fearing God; and whatsoever you do, do it heartily, as to the Lord, and not as unto man, knowing that of the Lord you shall receive the reward of the inheritance, for you serve the Lord Christ; but he that doeth wrong shall receive for the wrong which he hath done, and there is no respect of persons. Walk in wisdom toward them that are without religion, redeeming the time; let your speech be always with grace, seasoned with salt, that you may know how you ought to answer every man.

The various sinful habits and uncomelinesses remaining in our bodies naturally, being contrary to a strictly religious life, must be brought into subjection to the will of God, which is not hid any more from our eyes, although such were lying dormant for a little while, while we were in a glorified state of happiness and enjoyment on account of being set free from our sins, and the heavy burden which rested upon us for the sins and misdoings of the past, some of which have already been mentioned. Now the first thing Satan will bring up is, that all is naught and we are not saved, because we fail to accomplish that which we think we will do; thus the conflict will begin. We are now to begin to walk, and our walk is not in darkness, for

now we see, whereas before we were blind.
As we naturally see, when the child begins to
walk, it glories in it, but unexpectedly it
falls; the parent stretches forth the hand and
helps it up again, and the child proceeds as
before with joy; but soon it falls again, and
by and by it is hurt and becometh fretful,
and begins to fear the fall; but by the cheer-
ing of the parents, and the help offered, it
ventures on again and again, until it learns
to walk; and by exercise it not only gets
stronger, but gains courage to proceed. But
we must not forget that the child is fed and
nourished to become stronger in body all
this time it is thus exercised; and thus, when
we begin to walk with God in Christ, we do
not get very far until there is a fall or blun-
der made unexpectedly. We look up as if
something was about, and say, "Lord, forgive
me; this I will not again commit; I will
watch closely;" but it will not be long until
the same doth befall you; there will be

something else, perhaps worse than the first, and you begin to think about that which Satan told you, that you are not saved from sin. But pray on; look up to Christ; he is the father of the fatherless and as a husband to the widow; he will help you to overcome shortly, at least some of the things that are in your way, by which you will be encouraged. When the Israelites were bitten with the fiery serpents, they were ordered to look upon the brazen serpent which was put up on a pole, and they that did look up did not die, but they that did not look all died. Now, these failings are like the fiery serpents; they bite our souls, and we feel it; now we must likewise look up to Jesus, and shall not die. But now we go on, and one failing or misdoing follows another; we are bit and healed again and again, and the more we come short the worse we feel; it creates within us a great caution and strong resolution to withstand. Now not being able to accomplish that which we think must be done, we naturally and continually flee to the Lord for help, saying, "Lord, help, or I perish;" then we learn, and then only, the great truth, "without me you can do nothing." Then, as many and mighty things present themselves from time to time, Jesus will give us the power to overcome some of those things in which we so often had failed, and as completely as if we never had any trial with them. This, then, gives a sure testimony that we really have received the power from above; yes, so completely is sin under our power that we really are astonished when we think over the past—God himself hath really removed it out of our way. David said, "the testimonies of the Lord are sure, the testimonies of the Lord establish me." Now, while we are thus disciplined and trained for the eternal world to come, we have seasons when all is well, and we greatly rejoice in the peace and love of God, so

much so that we can say with the apostle to
be absent from the body, and present with
the Lord would be far better, knowing the
joys, sweetness and pleasantness of his presence ; and while we are thus contemplating,
he giveth us light to look around us, to see
the great work that is to be done, and that it
must be done by his servants in this world.
God in Christ Jesus maketh use of various
means, in the perfecting of his saints, by his
word and ministers from without, and by his
spirit within.

Now it becometh necessary for us to know
the judgment of God in Christ Jesus, and
with this judgment no man can judge but for
himself only. God spake through the prophet
enough for us to know and learn that we are
not able to judge one another with his judgment ; but as far as it is necessary for us to
judge, he hath laid down a judgment for us,
" By their fruits ye shall know them ; " and
this is the judgment he hath given unto us,

according to the seeing eye and the hearing
ear. But the judgment of God in Christ is
not so; he shall not judge according to the
seeing eye and the hearing ear, but righteous
judgment shall the Lord judge; a bruised
reed shall he not break, and a smoking flax
shall he not quench. Now from this judgment given unto man arise all our difficulties,
divisions and disputings, not considering the
judgment of God in Christ Jesus; and the
more so, when we consider our readiness to
judge others, taking the seat as judge, and
not considering what and who we are, but
considering ourselves as competent judges
for others; and not us only, but men who
live in sin and open rebellion against God.
Who that hath any eyes hath not seen this?
The Apostle Paul warned us much not to
judge one another; he saith, "Judge nothing
before the time is;" again, "What have I to
do with another's servant? to his master he
standeth or falleth, and he is able to hold him

up." Jesus saith, "Judge not, lest ye be judged; for with what judgment ye judge, you shall be judged, and with what measure ye mete, it shall be measured unto you again." Mercy is set against judgment, and he that sheweth no mercy shall have no mercy, and he that leadeth into captivity shall go into captivity.

And here is another mystery. All men have not the knowledge to use this world's goods; they have not the capacity to handle it; hence comes forth judgment unto condemnation by both parties. For instance, one man gathers money and makes money with it or out of it; the other man may have money, and make money beside that which he hath, and yet all is dead stock until it is all consumed and he becometh poor; and how shall he live a righteous life? But all appears to be in the hand of the Lord; for it is written, "It is an easy thing for the Lord to make the rich poor and the poor rich." One man's income is unsufficient for his expense, and he becometh poor, and another man's income overruns his expense, and though poor, he will become rich ; and both these men are religious, and deal honestly with their fellow-men. Now the man that becometh poor, or is poor from the beginning, if he doth not pay his honest debts, we condemn him as an unrighteous man, without regard to his willingness if he had the means to pay. The better class, if we may call them such, say he is no godly man, or he would not thus be lacking—amounting to what the apostle said, they think worldly gain is godliness. I have known sober and industrious men, who labored hard all their lifetime and raised a family, who began with nothing and when they died left less than nothing. (The Saviour said, the poor you will have always with you, and if you wish you can do them good, but me you will not have always.)

Then there are others who, Solomon said, will gather riches to their own hurt.

I will now endeavor to give you some experiences of my training in the service of the Lord. Not many years after my public conversion, there was a certain young man, who was held by all very high on account of his ability and grace, and Satan got the better of him so that he fell into an abominable sin, into which the young are most liable to fall. I never had such sympathy for any one in my life, and I prayed to God in great lamentation, asking God why he did not let me fall in his stead; that I was of no account to the church, and this man could not be spared; and as I was praying, humbling myself in ashes, the heaven above me opened, and these were the words that were spoken. *Those that keep my commandments will not fall into such things,* and all closed up again. I was frightened and got up from my knees; I did not need to ask, " who art thou ? " for

I knew it was the Lord. Now I could not ,pray for him any more in that manner ; but he hath repented long since, and whether he got to be the same useful man any more I cannot tell, for I have not seen him for many years.

The next I will relate was the transfiguration of this body; it was on a pentecostal day, or on a whitsuntide : I was away from home, waiting upon a woman, and there was much time ; and being far from home, I requested a room upstairs to myself, and while there alone, I lifted my eyes heavenward, and I was filled with the Holy Ghost, and was led out in the spirit, and was shown the many hardships that I must suffer, and fell into the hands of thieves and murderers ; at last I was delivered out of their hands, and soon I was on the summit of a large peak or hill, covered over with beautiful green grass. I was hardly right on the round top, when the heaven opened over my head, and the light of the glory of God came around me, and stood in great pillars all around the mount, me in the middle, the light still becoming more intense, until the green grass lost all its color, my hair, my hands and my clothes, became whiter than anything white I ever saw ; then the angels came marching with their music, and that was such music that no man can describe ; I had heard some of the best music that the world can afford or produce before, but it was as nothing at all to the angels' music on this occasion. Now I found myself falling or going upward (a great fear came over me, and yet I felt inexpressibly happy) ; I grasped hold of the grass, to hold myself from getting nearer to the presence of God. At this moment I was carried back into my room. Now when I found I was again in this world, the water rushed out of my eyes and ran down my cheeks in such a stream as it never did before nor since, because of my being again in this world of trouble and sorrow.

Years rolled on, and the weight and responsibility resting upon me in the various positions I held in the church, I thought I could no longer bear, as my body was giving way. I did not dare to exercise in public any more, on account of spitting blood, owing to straining of my lungs; and in much heaviness of mind, I prayed unto God to grant unto me leave of this branch of his household by a certain sign, and it was given. I withdrew and attached myself to another branch as a lay member, so that I would not have the burden of the church on me, but I was not long there until the Lord used me again as an instrument in his hands. But I was like ·Jonah, I would not go until he used his rod heavy on me (I knew if I were to attend to such matters that they would hate me); but at last I was compelled to go forward. I saw the bread cast unto the dogs, and the children wanting bread; so I attended unto small matters from time to time as the Lord gave, but in such a way that I should not become offensive unto them. The Lord not being well pleased, he took me into a vision, and thus it was like (on a beautiful evening, the moon shining bright). A man was kneeling in the clouds, with his face turned toward heaven, looking up; his left hand stretched up as if in the act of receiving something, but his right hand bent down as if in the act of making a desperate grasp of what is below. I told the vision unto them, and left them to judge for themselves. Not long after this, I was upon my bed, asleep; a voice in a loud tone said, "Know it is not the richest ground that grows the best wheat." I awoke and looked around the room to see who it was that spoke, but there was none in the room. I lived on for some time, still called upon to come and labor with my former companions in the Lord, but as I would not, the Lord visited me with a heavy scourge, took away my companion, and brought me down to the threshold of death; I expected to die, and suffered it patiently. Then one day as I was sitting in my chair, the word from the Lord came unto me, "Why will you thus die and not serve me?" I looked up, as it were, considering that I loved peace and my ease too well. I answered, "If thou wilt heal me, I will take up thy burden upon me again; but do thou give me strength to bear up under it." So he soon healed me, and I went to work again. Let all the world think and say what they please, I know whom I serve.

Solomon saith, he that increaseth knowledge increaseth sorrow, and you will find this to be true; for he that hath knowledge is like the rich man with gold; he is poor, yea very poor. My dear friend, if you undertake to draw nigh unto God, you must be in great fear and watchfulness; for our God is a

6

consuming fire to a sinner; God hath told by the prophet, that your sins and misdoings separate between you and your God.

SANCTIFICATION.

I will not say much at this place, but I will give the apostle's instruction: "God hath, from the beginning, chosen you to salvation, through the sanctification of the spirit and the belief of the truth." Then it appears it is the gift of God, through Christ offering himself up for us. Again, " Who will condemn ? it is the blood of Christ that sanctifieth." Then we say, we were born again, through the spirit and power of God; not by being persuaded by man, or by the will of man, nor from the fear of the punishment of the law, because this would be a legal repentance and would soon wear off; but by the love and power of God, because he first loved us, in that he did not cut us off, as we justly had deserved, and forgave us our sins.

It was he that gave us the power to believe the truth; it was he that sent the spirit of God to testify unto our spirit that we are delivered from our sins, and filled our hearts with the love of God, that we were made to cry out, " our Father and our God," and if he become our father, then are we his sons, born unto him and sanctified by the blood of Jesus Christ, who came into the world, suffered and died in our stead, and rose again for our justification, and liveth that we shall live also with him. Then, as the apostle said, we were chosen and sanctified from the beginning; but now we speak more particularly of what sanctification is. It is that work of grace, by which we are renewed after the image of God, set apart for his service, and enabled to die unto sin and live unto righteousness. It must be carefully considered in a twofold light; first as an inestimable privilege granted unto us from God (Thess. v. 23), and second, as an all-comprehensive duty, required of us by his holy word (Thess. iv. 3). It is distinguished from justification thus: Justification changes our state before God as a judge; sanctification changes our hearts and lives before him as a Father. Justification precedes, and sanctification follows. The surety, the righteousness of Christ imputed, is our justifying righteousness; but the grace of God implanted is the matter of our sanctification. Justification is done at once, sanctification is gradual; and yet justification and sanctification are inseparably connected in the promises of God (Rom. viii. 28, 30), in the covenant of grace (Heb. viii. 10, 12), in the doctrine and promise of the gospel (Acts v. 31), and in the experience of true believers (1 Cor. vi. 11). First, sanctification is a divine work, as already stated, and not begun or carried on by the power of man (Tit. i. 5–9); Second, it is a progressive work, and not perfected at once (Prov. iv. 18); Third, it is an internal work, not consisting in external profession or bare morality (Psalms lvi. 5) ; and fourth, it is necessary work, necessary as to the evidence of our state, the honor of our character, the usefulness of our lives, the happiness of our minds, and the eternal enjoyment of God's presence in a future world (Job iii. 3 ; Heb. xii. 14).

Sanctification is known, 1st, by a holy reverence (Neh. v. 5) ; 2d, by an earnest regard, or zeal (Sam. iii. 24); 3d, by patient submission (Psalms xxxix. 9) ; sanctification is nothing less, than for a man to be brought to entire resignation to the will of God, and to offer up his soul as a whole burnt-offering to Christ ; 4th, it is known by an increased hatred to sin (Psalms cxix. 133) ; 5th, by communion with God (Isa. xxi. 8); 6th, by a delight in his word and ordinances (Psalms xxvii. 4) ; 7th, by humility (Job, xlii. 5, 6) ; 8th, by holy confidence (Psalms xxvii. 4) ;

9th, by praise to God (Psalms ciii. 1); and
10th, by uniform obedience (John xv. 8.)

There are certain duties imposed upon us,
which are acceptable before God and with
man; for if there be first a willing mind,
it is accepted according that a man hath,
and not to that which he hath not; for I
mean not that others be eased and you bur-
dened, but now at this time, that your
abundance may be a supply to their wants,
that there may be an equality among you, and
that you may help each other in the time of
need. As it is written, he that gathered
much had nothing over, and he that gathered
little had no lack; so then it is the duty of
the people of God to be in union, and not a
brother with evil heart go out among world-
lings with his dealings, and forsake his
brother, because he is required to deal justly
with him, or fall into the counsel of the
brethren. How often do we see this done!
It is nothing short of casting your bread unto

dogs, and letting the children want; it is not love, which scripture bids you to love in deed; but will you rather love in word only, and lose your soul through much covetousness? Be careful; the judgment of God is according to the intents and desires of the heart; there is nothing hid or in secret that shall not be made manifest in the day of the Lord. Some brethren of different denominations have told me, that they would rather deal with outsiders or sinners than with their brethren, on account of false brethren, who will accuse you, no matter how you deal with them; I say, let them be admonished to walk in the fear of God, and suffer with them, that they may be saved in the end; because our work is with God through Christ to save sinners, (and if there is love undefiled no one will suffer beyond measure,) and not to be bitter against them, but have charity, which hopeth all things, believeth all things, and endureth all things. It is easy to lose that which thou hast, if there be a willing mind; and that which thou hast not, thou canst not lose. Again, it may be permitted for thy trial; and shalt thou prove thyself unworthy? He that doeth wrong shall receive reward of the Lord, but pray for him that God will not mete out a severe punishment; for I tell you, if thou art true, God will draw the rod across him speedily; experience hath taught me this. The Saviour said, Be ye therefore wise as serpents and harmless as doves; Solomon saith, Let us hear the conclusion of the whole matter. Fear God and keep his commandments, for God shall bring every work unto judgment, with every secret thing, whether it be good or whether it be evil. Again, the Lord hath shewed thee, O man, what is good; and what doth the Lord require of thee, but to do justly, and love mercy, and walk humbly with thy God? Now concerning the doctrine of Christ, the Saviour said, If any man will do the will of God, he shall know of the doctrine whether it be of God, or whether I speak of myself.

In the discipline and training for the eternal world, we find some things which we have in our power to do, while there are others for which we must have the power from God through Christ, or we cannot do them. These are things which we can do: if thy right eye offend thee, pluck it out and cast it from thee, for it is profitable for thee that one of thy members should perish, and not thy whole body be cast into hell; and if thy right hand offend thee, cut it off and cast it from thee, for it is profitable for thee that one of thy members should perish, and not thy whole body should be cast into hell; and if thy right foot offend thee, cut it off and cast it from thee, for it is profitable for thee that one of thy members should perish, and not thy whole body be cast into hell. When doth our eye offend us? When we look upon the things we naturally desire to have, on that which is appreciable in the sight of man or the worldly mind, and is not becoming to a true Christian. We read, and Christ teaches us, that which is high and appreciable in the eyes of man is an abomination unto God ; then we see such things are offensive, and we have it in our power not to get it.   Now there is self-denial for us, not to allow ourselves the pleasure, because it is displeasing to God ; thus the eye is plucked out and cast away. Now, if I obey this not, what is the difference between me and the one which is under the curse and wrath of God, who hath the threatening of God to be cast into hell, if he turn not from his idols? No man is in Christ Jesus any further than he obeys.   The right hand in the same way ; it only becometh the right and foremost hand, when it reacheth for the things it should not ; it is naturally ready to receive, but not so ready to give (although it is written it is more blessed to give than to receive), and not only thus, but even ready to receive that which belongeth unto others; and thus it becometh offensive according to the inner man. This must be denied; this kind of a hand must be cut off and cast away; for we are required to deal justly, and do that which is right before God and man. Likewise our foot becometh the right foot, when according to the natural inclinations it would walk to places where the ungodly have their pastime and enjoyment—to places where God is not glorified, and where we are made no better fitted for heaven. Here then is a self-denial; this foot must be cut off and cast from us. All these things in an outward way we have in our power to prevent, and please God in all these things. He that glories, let him glory in the Lord; for if we are crucified unto the world and the world is crucified unto us, how shall we have pleasure and pastime among sinners, except in their salvation? And there are the ordinances of our Lord and Saviour, which are in our power to do (and that I might be of advantage unto those who desire the whole truth, all theologians or learned men in Scripture agree, that where the precept is given and the example shown, such shall be done to the honor and glory of God in Christ). Now after repentance, for then only can we believe, water baptism is the first. In this we have the precept and example of our Saviour, that it was a righteousness to be fulfilled, representing washing and cleansing, and that in the water ; for the first one hundred years, no one knew anything else, nor attempted to change the practice. The breaking and eating of bread, we also have by precept and example ; " This is my body that is broken for you ;" the wine cup by precept and example, " Take, drink ye all of it ; this is my blood that is shed for many, for the remission of sins ;" and the washing of feet, by precept and example, to remember his humility in coming into the flesh ; " As oft as you do this, do it in remembrance of me." Now, these things are in our power to do. So far as it concerns us externally, to what benefit ? Much every way, because he established them for us to be exercised thereby ; but they that are wise in themselves, unlearned and unstable, wrest these, as they do also many 'other Scriptures, to their own damnation, as Peter hath said. Now these things we say are in our power to do, to prevent evil and fulfill many outward things ; but it takes nothing less than the power of God to quench internal evil, and fulfill in our souls and spirits the proper thing. The apostle includes the whole matter under three heads to be overcome by the Christian ; the lust of the eye, the lust of the flesh and the pride of life ; and these appear to be burning fires in man. Thus we find men who have become so habituated and hardened, that they must by prayer receive from God the power to overcome and eradicate themselves from those strong and wrong-formed habits.

Then again there are many things that we have no power at all, as in saving one another, etc.; but this we have got, we can tell each other of our exercise in the work, and thereby encourage each other, and instruct each other; which I find of great benefit, because of our short-mindedness, and forgetfulness, through our engagement in temporal duties, which must be carried along; as it is written, "He that provideth not for his own household hath denied the faith and is worse than an infidel;" again, "He that laboreth not, shall not eat;" we shall not eat the bread of idleness.

CONSCIENCE.

Conscience signifies knowledge in conjunction with the facts to which it is a witness, as the eye is to the action done before it; a double or joint knowledge, namely, of a divine law or rule. It is that part of the soul that will remain for ever. Conscience has been considered first natural, or that common principle which instructs men of all countries and religions in the duties to which they are all alike obligated. There seems to be something of this in the minds of all men, even in the darkest regions of the earth, and among the rudest tribes of men; a distinction has ever been made between just and unjust, a duty and a crime. Second, a right conscience is that which decides aright, or according to the only rule of rectitude, the law of God; this is a well-informed conscience, which in all its decisions proceeds upon the most evident principle of truth. Third, a probable conscience is that which admits of the brightest and fullest light, and contents itself with probabilities; the consciences of many are of no higher character. Fourth, an ignorant conscience, or that which declares aright, but as it were by chance, without any just ground to build upon. Fifth, an erroneous conscience, is a conscience mistaken in its decision about the nature of actions; and how strong do we see men in this kind of conscience!—yes, so strong as to risk the loss of their own souls, by not paying strict attention to all that God hath said. Sixth, a double conscience, unresolved about the nature of things and actions, on account of the nearly equal probabilities which appear for and against each side of the question. Seventh, an evil conscience, in regard to actions generally; it is evil when it has lost more or less the sense it ought to have of the natural distinctions of moral good and evil; this is a deluded or defiled conscience—when reflecting upon wickedness it feels no pain—it is evil, and said to be seared or hardened. 1 Tim. iv. 2; it is also evil when during the commission of sin it lies quiet; in regard to future actions, it is evil if it doth not startle at the proposal of sin.

A good rule is, keep the love of God in your soul; which you cannot do unless you keep all that which he hath told you, as far as is in your power to do, and that only will preserve you a pure conscience; for he that loveth God will keep his sayings, and there is no further conscience need be established. But conscience can be defiled; trust it not without the word of God; look at the men that cast themselves under the car of Juggernaut, how strong their conscience is! But, you say, I have a good conscience toward God; I know that he hath pardoned my transgressions and hath forgiven my sins. I say, can he deny that which he hath promised? If thou come and confess thy sins, he will forgive them, and whenever and as often as thou comest in the way he hath appointed. But, O man, dost thou not consider that he is also a just God, and will hold a final reckoning with you? and will not your condemnation be only the greater, when thou hast much received and hast nothing in the end? Thus if we continually receive and bury it with sin again, and not put to usury, but consume it in our lusts as we go along, what will we have at the final settlement, when we shall give an account of that which we have received, and have nothing to show? Will he say, " Thou hast been faithful over little, I will set thee over much?" I trow not. On the other hand, have we become better men, more useful in the world, and a shining light and help to his cause? Have we become truly honest before God and man? Have we become more righteous in our dealings with our fellowman, and learned to speak the truth at all times? Have we made a proper use of the privileges and means, that we have so long enjoyed, to learn that which we must do to stand the final test? Or have we lived heedless and careless, and drifted along with the world when outside of the church walls, and not improved our talent, but enjoyed ourselves in the things of this world, forgetting God? Do we not see, he that overcomeeth shall inherit all things? He did overcome, and promised the power unto us, that we shall also overcome these things. Now to what purpose are a set of carpenter's tools, if he doth not make use of them? So likewise is Christ unto us, if we do not make use of his promised power, and the means he hath appointed for us to be exercised in. "Yes, but I have a hope, a good hope." The sinner and the wicked hath a hope also; but the hope of the wicked shall perish, it shall not stand. There are only four actual steps down to hell, and how natural it goeth! The first is debt, the second is lying, the third is stealing, and the fourth is murder.

Now in conclusion I would simply add, that the Scripture and our experience in these exercises must correspond and agree together, and that not a certain part or portion; man is so apt to select such passages as will carry him out in the principle he hath built upon, but the whole matter must be reconciled, or our foundation will not stand the test in that great day. That our discipline and training may be the better understood, the child of God is born a child and groweth up to a youth, then to a man, and then to an old father and mother in Christ. In a natural point of view we see these facts, but in a spiritual point of view we have not; at least I, for one, have not yet come to that old age that I desire. The apostle said, Not that I have attained to it, but I run after it that I may attain to it. Let me caution myself and all, what the Saviour said, "He that hath my commandments and keepeth them, he it is that loveth me." Now be it known that we are all naturally very uneven, and if we really see this, we put no confidence in ourselves, lest our eyes be closed and our knowledge become lacking; but let us search, pray and trust in the Lord, and walk in his ways, which must alone be the rule of our life; than it matters not what this man doeth, or what this or that one may think or say, the whole course lies between me and my God, and between you and your God—it is strictly personal, for every one shall render his or her own account, and not one for another.   See, I have told you as a faithful servant; therefore the things which are in our power to do, let us do them without missing one, for he that is guilty of one is guilty of the whole, saith the Lord; and as we pass along he will give unto us the sure testimony of his aid and love.   And let us add to our faith virtue, and to virtue knowledge, and to knowledge temperance, and to temperance patience, and to patience godliness, and to godliness brotherly kindness, and to brotherly kindness charity; for if these things be in us and abound, they will make us that we will neither be barren nor unfruitful in the knowledge of our Lord Jesus Christ; but he

that lacketh these things is blind and cannot
see afar off, and hath forgotten that he was
purged from his old sins; but if we do these
things we shall never fall.   Therefore let us
be diligent to make our calling and election
sure, that we may enter the kingdom of our
Lord and Saviour Jesus Christ; let us love all
men alike with the love of God, for he maketh no difference.   God is love, and he that
abideth in love abideth in God and God
abideth in him.   The grace of our Lord and
Saviour Jesus Christ, the love of God, and the
communion of the Holy Ghost, rest and
abide with you all, Amen.

To the work, to the work, we are servants of
    God;
Let us follow the path our Master hath trod;
With the balm of his counsel our strength to
    renew,
Let us do with our might what our hands find
    to do.
        Toiling on, toiling on,

Toiling on, toiling on,
Let us hope, let us watch,
And labor till the Master comes.

There are yet many things that I might write about, but I mean to stir up your minds to go to work ; because it is not so much to know, as it is to work. But, how shall or will you work, if you do not know him for whom you are to work ? Therefore read and think, and read this book again and again, and reflect upon its words.

HEAVEN.

That there is a future state of happiness, both reason and Scripture indicate, and a general notion of happiness after death hath had its existence among the wiser sort of heathen, who had only the light of nature to guide them. If we examine the human mind there is a natural desire of happiness in **all** men, and which, it is equally evident, is **not** attainable in this life.

Heaven must be considered as a place as
well as a state; it is expressly so termed in
Scripture, John xiv. 2, 3, and the existence
of the body of Christ, and those of Enoch
and Elijah, is a further proof of it.   We believe it is above; as some say, above the
starry heaven; we are called upon to look up,
where Christ sitteth at the right hand of
God; Christ lifted his eyes up at the grave of
Lazarus, and on various other occasions, and
also said, I came from above, I am from
above, etc.

Heaven, however, we are assured, is a
place of inexpressible felicity.   The names
given are proofs of this; it is called Paradise,
Luke xxiii. 43; light, Rev. xxi. 23; a building and mansion of God, 2 Cor. xv. 1; John
xiv. 2; a better country, Heb. xi. 16; a
kingdom, Matt. xxv. 34; an inheritance,
Acts xx. 23; a crown, 2 Tim. iv. 8; glory,
Psalms lxxxiv. 11 ; peace, rest and joy of the
Lord, Isa. lvii. 2; Heb. iv. 9 ; Matt. xxv.

21, 23, etc. The happiness and joy of heaven will consist in freedom from all evil, both of body and of soul, Rev. vii. 17; the full enjoyment of God, as a chief good, in the company of angels. We will be seated around the tables spread with angels' food, and Christ the Lord will gird himself and wait upon us as his guests, etc. Now, there are many suppositions of men, that are really of no service unto us; whether there will be a different language spoken, and if not, which shall be the language; some say the Hebrew, because it is the language always used by God; and whether we shall know each other according to the flesh. If this can be of any benefit unto you, and you can receive it, we shall have no mortal knowledge, because this mortality shall put on immortality, and this corruptible shall put on incorruption. The Saviour said, they neither marry nor are given in marriage, but are like the angels; therefore this earthly love that binds us together, as fathers, mothers, brothers, sisters, husbands and wives, parents and children, together with all our worldly knowledge and distinctions, will remain in the earth, for they are earthly, and earth cannot exist in heaven, also it would be no place of enjoyment and happiness. But the love of God in the soul will abide forever, together with the immortal love of the saints; for the love of God constrains us to love his redeemed. Now we have a foretaste of it, when we consider with what kind of love we love them that are no kin unto us according to the flesh; for the love of God drowns this earthly love, and this proves it: when we see our sons and daughters converted to God, and filled with the spirit of God, what a different kind of love enters into our souls, if so be that we walk according to the spirit and not according to the flesh. Let this be sufficient, to know that we shall be where we wish to be, have all things that we desire to have, be among the most desirable company, hear that which is the most pleasant to hear, see that which is the most pleasing to the eye, and have a feeling that is inexpressibly good, namely the full presence of God, in all his majesty and glory, of the which some of us, at least, had a slight foretaste in this world. On one occasion God did show unto me what it is to be delivered from this body: I was not in this mortal body, but, as it were, this mortal body was left by itself at a certain place, and I was at another place, and I had such sweet communion with God as is far beyond expression. There was no earthly thought, or knowledge, neither remembrance of anything to interfere, but a full and entire enjoyment with God—such felicity that is indescribable by any man. The death of the man of God is equally so, when we shall be finally and eternally delivered from this mortal body   This hath been shewed unto me. The death of this mortal body we naturally

more or less dread, and especially so when
we see the struggle of the spirit to get disen-
tangled and loosened from the body of our
fellow man in death; the very appearance
bringeth a deep feeling of awe and gloom
on us; but now rest assured, all ye children
of the living God, if you have lived in the
Lord ye shall die in the Lord; there will be
such a pleasure in your hour of death, when
God holds out the crown of glory. What a
different and unexpected feeling there will
be! (It is the remorse of conscience that
maketh death so terrible.) Lift up your
heads, for your redemption draweth nigh,
namely, the deliverance from this mortal
body. Suffice it to say, we shall be seated
around the tables spread with angels' food in
the paradise of God, and Christ will gird
himself and serve us (as he said). Amen.

HELL.

This is the place of divine punishment after death. As all religions have supposed a future state of existence after this life, all have their hell, or place of punishment or torment, in which the wicked are to be punished. Even the heathens have their Tartara, and the Mahometans we find believe in future rewards and punishments;—it is not, therefore, a sentiment peculiar to Christianity. There have been many peculiar conjectures, respecting the place of the damned, which will be useless for us to think or write about.   As to the nature of this punishment, we may form some idea from scriptural passages, expressed so that we shall dread to get there. It is called a place of torment, Luke xvi. 21; the bottomless pit, Rev. xx. 3–6; a prison, 1 Peter iii. 19; darkness, Matt. viii. 12; Jude 13; fire, Matt. xiii. 42–50; a worm that never dies, Mark ix. 44–48; the second

death, Rev. xxi. 8 ; the wrath of God, Rom.
ii. 5.   Whether there will be material fire, I
leave for others to judge; but it is written by
some that the wicked shall have their place,
where devils howl and the damned spirits
take up their doleful lamentations.   But let
this suffice us : we are sure it is the opposite
of heaven, where those unfortunates shall get
that which they most hate, see that which is
the most horrifying to behold, hear that
which of all is the most distressing to hear,
feel that which is insufferable, and be among
the company most undesirable and abominable ; and this altogether will produce a horrible feeling and suffering that is worse than
death to the sinner; for it is written that
the wicked gnaw their tongues for pain,
and seek for death to find release, but death
fled from them; yea, they shall search and
seek for death like a man seeks for a pearl,
but they shall not find it.   But we say there
is less necessity for us to know all about the

place, and its peculiar torments, and all its
abominable things, than there is for us to
know how to live to avoid getting there.
Christ hath made ample provision for us;
now to make proper use of these means
requires our serious consideration. May God
help us and give us the grace! Thank God,
through Jesus Christ we can escape.

LITURGY.

I am not so much opposed to a liturgy as
some are, because God hath his particular
order and form laid down for man to go by,
and the first rule of heaven is order. The
apostle said, Let all things be done in order.
Some churches have their prayers in writing,
and their members are required to read them
off, so that the unlearned do not make vain
repetitions in their prayers. It is true we
shall all be taught of God, but all things are
not accomplished at once in a child. Not-
withstanding, all men know that a prayer of

words only is mockery; that is, if the feeling, wants and desires are not with it. Now it is my desire to teach and be taught in all things that are good unto edification, so that I may stand acquitted in the day of the Lord. As I have given you some of my experience, I will give you some concerning this matter also, in my discipline and training for the eternal world. In regard to the exercise in prayer; when we are in private prayer, we ask for those things we stand in need of and also for our fellow-man, namely, the grace or power of God through Christ, to overcome the evils and sins that surround us; but when we pray in public we are governed by the particular circumstances, so that one particular form of prayer will not answer in all places and at all times. In public prayer let us observe the same order that we do in singing; let every person's mind follow the prayer that is spoken in public, so that all men may say amen, and not one crying out this and another that, with such a confused noise that sinners cannot understand the petition offered up; God would not allow me this from my beginning, no matter how poor the one was in words that led in prayer. May God grant you, reader, to know that God observes strict order in all things, and that if you will ask him he will instruct you in all things that are acceptable in his sight— at least if there be a willing mind to learn for yourself, and not follow the example of others, who make a great adulation in the church, and without the church walls are such as we frequently see. Follow not their example, but pray God that they may be saved. I will give you my private prayer as God taught me, when I asked him to teach me how to pray, and what for to pray; and it hath not got old yet to this day, although I often lack the feeling desirable, as we often do in all prayers, namely, that of the poor in spirit. But of such the promise is given, he

8

that receives not the kingdom of heaven **as a** little child, cannot enter into it, are **the** words of the Saviour.

Private Form.

I thank thee, my heavenly Father, for **thy** long suffering, patience, goodness and mercy, and loving kindness, which thou hast not only extended toward thy poor and degraded little ones, but toward all the children of man; and especially in the gift of thy Son, that all may turn unto thee and have everlasting life.

I implore thee, that thou wilt remember those which are not so highly favored as I **am** (in this morning, noon, or evening hour, etc.), who are laid down on beds of affliction, suffering with pain of body and distraction of mind, and cannot come before thee to speak a word unto thee, or even to think of thee, as I can. Oh! give me a thankful heart, that it is as well with me yet as **it is,** and let them know that thou art the giver of every good and perfect gift, the helper in the time of need, the comforter in the time of sore distress, and the strength in the time of extreme weakness.

Such as are old and enfeebled, whose day of life hath been spent, the eventide of death drawn nigh, body and mind become weak and enfeebled, O let the sun of righteousness shine upon them, bright, even as a noontide sun shineth, that they may still rest and abide in thy works and thee, and thou in them, such as are at the moment of exit of time, whose doom will forever be sealed, O let thy rod and thy staff guide and comfort them through the valley and shadow of death, that they may be safely landed over into the eternal world of happiness and glory.

Kings, rulers and governors of land and sea, city and town, over this wide world, give them wise hearts, that they may so rule this world, that thy people may still have a peaceable waiting before thee, without any interference on their part from without ; give them also to know that they have a heaven to gain and a hell to shun, and thee to glorify.

Have mercy upon thy people everywhere, and give us the things that are needful ; eyes that we might see aright, ears that will hear, a heart to understand, a tongue that can speak to thee, hands that will labor in thy vineyard, and feet that will walk in the path of rectitude ; the wisdom and knowledge to know thy will, and the power to do it. Herein hear, O Father, lest thy people should perish.

Such as are the shepherds of the flock, the work and the power is in your hands and so are we ; have mercy upon us, give us that bread from heaven which is bread indeed, and that water of life that is drink indeed, that thy people may be so fed and nourished, as to grow up from childhood to youth, from youth to manhood, and from manhood to old fathers and mothers in Christ Jesus. O, Saviour, save thy people and bless thy inheritance.

Such as are strangling in birth, who have the umbilical cord of this world wrapped around their necks, and cannot breathe the free air, O have mercy upon them, and let them know that every high and appreciable thing of this world is an abomination in thy sight. O, let their minds be far elevated above the fleeting things of this life ; let them not perish, but rescue them from danger, that they may be saved through the blood of the covenant.

The wise of this world, who by their wisdom and knowledge construe thy doctrine so as to make some null and void, and replenish things which thou hast not bidden, to bring an abomination before thy face, let them know that every man is but foolish, and that thou art only wise, and the words which thou hast spoken shall judge a man at the last day. O, let them not be taken in the day of judgment by surprise, but rescue them from danger, that they may be saved.

The innumerable multitude, living in the world without knowing thee, seeking thee little and caring less, let the day be speedily brought about when they may turn unto the overtures of mercy, and eventually be saved through the blood of the covenant.

Thy poor and degraded little ones, give us a heart that we might in truth say, Our Father, who art in heaven, hallowed be thy name, thy kingdom come, thy will be done in earth as it is in heaven (O, give us the power that such may be fully done); give us this day our daily bread, and forgive us our trespass as we forgive those that trespass against us (give us that forgiving heart, that we may forgive as we wish to be forgiven), and lead us not into temptation, but deliver us from evil, for thine is the kingdom, and the power, and the glory forever (and remaineth with thee). Amen.

Now the foregoing I have not obtained or acquired from books and much study, all the principal thought hath been obtained through much prayer and exercise in prayer in secret, for the wants of myself and others—asking God to teach me, as I found that I was a child in knowledge and deed, and that the true Christian instruction must come from God, who only is wise. Learning the letter is good, but the true understanding usefulness must be obtained by prayer; and this that I have written often proved manna to my soul in dark seasons. It doth not seem to be getting old, it proves unto me always fresh and of benefit; therefore have I put it in writing, and my brother, if God hath learned you a better exercise for private devotion, all right; but of this I am certain: the man that repeats this prayer in secret three times a day, with the proper desire and understanding of the heart, and attends to the means of grace otherwise, will not be unfruitful in the work and knowledge of the Lord.

Family Evening Exercise.

Now all the day has passed by,
  The sun doth no more shine,
We leave wherein we've labored lie,
  And sorrows, tears and pine.

O, Lord be pleased to think of me,
  In this dark and dreary night,
And let me thy protection see,
  The power of thy might.

Should this prove the last night for me,
  And end my earthly care,
Then take me into heaven with thee,
  The saints' glories to share.

After singing the above, we have the following prayer:

Our Heavenly Father, we thank thee for thy merciful preservance and care which thou hast extended toward us during the past day, until this evening hour; be thou further merciful this night, and take us into thy care. We submit our life, soul, and body into thy hands; deal thou according to thy justly extolled mercy, and preserve us from all evil and harm. Bless us that we may rejoice in thy glorious majesty, and in nothing else; bless also our neighbors, friends and enemies around us, and preserve them in much mercy until the day it may please thee to draw them into thy ways and to do thy will; and such as are sick and afflicted, and are not able to rest as we do, make their sufferings easy, and let them know that thou dost draw them unto thee, to submit to thy will, and to suffer thy ways. Lord, be thou with thy people, lead and guide us through this life, and in death save us, for Christ's sake. Amen.

Family Morning Exercise.

Our morning exercise is prayer only:

Our Heavenly Father, we thank thee for thy merciful preservation and care which thou hast extended toward us during the past night, until this morning hour. Be thou further merciful this day, and take us into thy care; our bodies, and keep them from evil deeds, our minds from evil thoughts, and our tongues from evil speaking.   Let thy spirit rest and abide with us, that we may walk in thy ways, do thy will, and praise thy holy name both by act and by deed. Bless us with that heavenly blessing that we may rejoice in thy glorious majesty, and in nothing else. Bless also our neighbors, friends and enemies, around us; let them know that they live of thy goodness and mercy, and preserve them in much mercy until the day it may please thee to draw them into thy ways and to do thy will.   And those that are of the household of faith, be thou powerful upon us with thy spirit, remove every obstacle out of the way, comfort the comfortless, strengthen the weak, lead and guide us through this life in such a way as to fit us out for thy kingdom above, through Christ our Redeemer. Amen.

Giving of Thanks at Meal-Time.

I will give you my first form that the spirit of thought presented at the time, which was afterward amended, as I felt it more edifying to those around me. While we are eating before the Lord, if so be that we are in the Lord, it would require no words on our part; but to teach others who know not God, it is necessary that we should pray aloud for their good. To pray both before and after meals is superfluous, except for those who, while eating, forget that they are before God; such may well pray for forgiveness of their sins committed while eating. But this I say, be not discouraged if the rod of the Lord be heavily drawn across your back when you pray or speak in public or before men, so as to make things pleasant to their minds;—then consider what thou hast done that was not pleasing to God.

First Form : We thank thee, our Heavenly Father, for the blessing which thou hast left before us again, and we are unworthy of it. O do thou let that heavenly blessing come within our reach, which we so much more need than the present, for Christ's sake. Amen.

Second Form : We thank thee, our Heavenly Father, for the blessing which thou hast left before us again, and we are unworthy of it. Sanctify a portion of what is before us to its intended use, and us to thy service, and in heaven save us, for Christ's sake. Amen.

Third Form : All eyes wait upon thee, O God. Thou givest meat to the hungry and drink to the thirsty in due season; by thy hands are all the living filled with thy blessing. Give us grateful hearts to enjoy what is before us; ever feed our souls with that bread from heaven, and finally save us in thy kingdom, for Christ's sake. Amen.

In conclusion, if you are really converted to God, I would say with Samuel the Prophet, do as occasion serves thee, for the Lord is

with thee. . But bear in mind that Saul the
king lost his kingdom, for not closely observ-
ing the word of the Lord, in sparing the
king and some fine cattle, which he was
utterly to destroy and to spare not; but he
had mercy on his enemy without God's per-
mission, and thereby made himself offensive;
and again when he was commanded to wait
seven days until Samuel the Prophet would
come down to sacrifice, before going unto
battle with the Philistines, Samuel did not
come at the appointed time, and Saul became
frightened at the enemy and offered up a
sacrifice, which was not in his place to do;
he did not trust in God, and thus did prove
himself before God that he did not fully rely
on God. As it was to try him, so God will
let his people be tried; and if we be found
faithful, it shall be for our credit. Job said,
Though thou slay me, yet will I trust in thee.
Wait patiently upon the Lord and trust in
him, and in the end thou shalt more than

conquer. What you do, do it with your might, and observe order strictly. Have thy prayers suitable to the occasion (not praying for saint and sinner when thou art to give thanks to God at meal time), in a few words, and that to the point, which is pleasing to God and man. A long prayer at meal time is out of order entirely. Christ thanked God, then gave, or broke the bread, as they used no knives to cut it. And at all times, a very long prayer hath many vain repetitions, which hath been forbidden. Beside all this, the very act shows it to be a prayer of words only, like the priests in the time of Elias—they prayed a whole day without avail, but Elias used only a few words suited to the occasion, and the fire came down and consumed the sacrifice.

God bless you, and give you an understanding heart. Amen.

THE END.

Lightning Source UK Ltd.
Milton Keynes UK
UKHW011941021218
333216UK00013B/2142/P